Terrance Talks Travel: The Quirky Tourist Guide to Marrakesh

Terrance Zepke

All queries should be directed to: www.safaripublishing.net.

For more about the author, visit www.terrancezepke.com and www.terrancetalkstravel.com.

Library of Congress Cataloging-in-Publication Data

ISBN: 978-1-942738-51-0

Zepke, Terrance

Terrance Talks Travel: The Quirky Tourist Guide to Marrakesh

1. Travel-Morocco. 2. Adventure Travel. 3. Marrakesh. 4. Marrakech. 5. Travel-Middle East. Travel-North Africa. 7. Marrakesh Guidebook. 9. The Medina-Djemaa El-Fna. 10. Marrakesh Attractions. 11. Sahara Desert. 12. Casablanca. 13. Fez. I. Title.

First edition

Safari Publishing

CONTENTS

INTRODUCTION

Recently, Marrakesh has become a favorite destination for adventure travelers and backpackers. Adventure travelers are thrilled at all there is to see and do in and around this ancient city. Backpackers love how far their dollars and euros will go.

I was trying to think of how to describe to Marrakesh in this introduction when I was overwhelmed with all the things that popped into my head.

That's because Marrakesh is an eclectic mix of ancient cultures, arts, architecture, and adventure. It is a bustling, thriving, frenetic place filled with fortune tellers, snake charmers, storytellers, henna ladies, colorful souks, singular hammams and riads, extraordinary mosques, remarkable museums, distinctive gardens, huge palm groves, and much more!

Marrakesh is one of the oldest and most charming cities in Morocco. It is my favorite city. Casablanca was disappointing. It was just another big city with lots of high rises. It was not at all what I was expecting. Fes was all right, but it is also a city that's a bit too big, and its claim to fame is all its foul-smelling tanneries.

But Marrakesh is just right. Its 1,000 years of history includes epic battles, empires, imperialism, sultans, sharifs, harems, sheikhs, and Berbers. With its Arab and North Africa influences, Marrakesh is the best of Morocco. And it is the perfect place for the quirky traveler.

You will explore royal tombs, picturesque palaces, ancient ruins, and historic medinas. But Marrakesh is not about tours and tourist attractions. While it has plenty of these things, it's about the senses. You will *smell* many aromas, including exotic spices and dyes. You will *see* chaotic medinas, narrow alleys and labyrinths full of colorful souks, donkey carts, tuk tuks, and young men racing through town on scooters. You will *hear* the call of prayer and vendors begging you to come see their wares. You will *feel* welcome and a bit awestruck in Marrakesh.

Read on to discover some amazing adventures, exciting experiences, and intriguing places. Get ready for a Moroccan adventure of a lifetime…

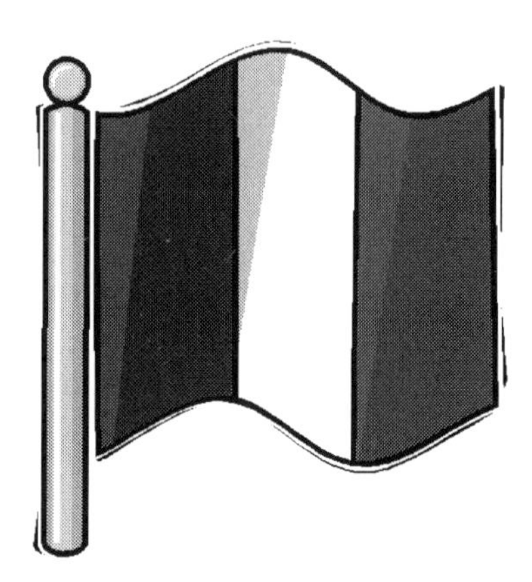

FYI: Marrakesh is the English spelling while Marrakech is the accepted French spelling. France once conquered Morocco, so that influence is still prevalent throughout Morocco, especially in Marrakesh. More than half of the population speaks French and many signs are written in French. Their outstanding infrastructure is largely thanks to France. French colonization had a big, positive impact on the Kingdom of Morocco.

GETTING THERE & GETTING AROUND

Morocco is located in northern Africa. Border countries include Algeria, Spain, and Western Sahara.

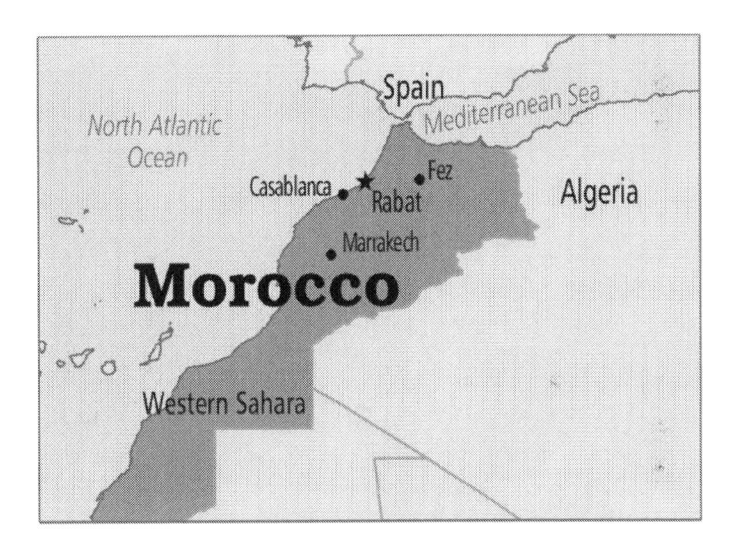

<u>DISTANCE FROM MARRAKESH TO…</u>

Sydney, Australia=11,238 miles
Johannesburg, South Africa=7,581 miles
Delhi (India)=6,385 miles
Lima, Peru=5,481 miles
New York City, New York=3,643 miles
Cairo, Egypt=3,043 miles
London, England=1,879 miles
Paris, France=1,596 miles
Lisbon, Spain=816 miles

By Air

There are many airlines that offer international flights into Marrakesh. However, British Airways, Ryanair, Iberia, KLM, Lufthansa, Air France, and EasyJet offer the most flights. The lowest fares are typically found on EasyJet and Ryanair. They fly into **Marrakech-Menara Airport**. The airport is ten to fifteen minutes from the center of Marrakesh. You will need a passport and will have to fill out an embarkation card to present upon arrival, but no visas are required. http://www.onda.ma/en/Our-Airports/Marrakech-Ménara-Airport.

For airport transfers, the bus or a taxi is the best way to go. The bus is very cheap and the taxi is a fixed fare for the two-mile ride from the airport to Old Town.

FYI: Watch your step. There are donkeys, carriages, vehicles, motorcycles, bicycles, and scooters everywhere in the city. Use caution when crossing the street!

By Land

If you're planning on driving to Marrakesh, that is a viable option. It is about a six-hour drive from Fez or 2 ½ hours from Casablanca. It is fairly easy and safe to navigate all of Morocco except for within the city limits of Fez where driving and parking is a challenge. That said, driving rules in Morocco are loose, to say the least. The lines dictating lanes mean very little. People drive fast and seemingly reckless. Honking means many things, such as getting ready to pass you, in the process of passing you, you're not going fast enough (you will also be aggressively tailgated), or any number of other reasons. Watch out for donkeys, camels, and goats crossing the road or on the road. As you enter a town, be aware that locals often congregate on or close to the road. They seem oblivious to traffic. Be prepared for delays and some road chaos and you'll be fine. Oh, and you need to be able to drive a manual (stick shift), as there are few automatics in Morocco. Technically, you need an International Driver's License to drive in Morocco, but no one asks to see it, including the police and rental car agencies. However, if you want to be on the safe side, you can get one through AAA. And just like in the U.S., there are speed traps, so pay attention to other drivers and you'll quickly learn when and where to slow down. You could simply go the speed limit consistently, but you will probably get run over if you do so!

More Options

Morocco is less than ten miles south of Spain. **High speed ferries** rip across the Strait of Gibraltar to reach Tangier, Morocco in less than thirty minutes. From there, you can take a train, bus, or car to Marrakesh. https://www.frs.es/en/

FYI: Tangier is the oldest city in Morocco.

The **trains** are operated by ONCF. They have routes to all the major cities, including Marrakesh. You can choose first or second class tickets. Second class tickets are cheap, so this is a great option. https://www.oncf.ma/en/

If traveling by train from London, Paris, or Madrid, here is what you can expect:

London to Paris by Eurostar (train)⟶Paris to Madrid by Trainhotel Elipsos (train)⟶Madrid to Algeciras by Altaria (train)⟶Ferry from Algeciras to Tangier⟶Tangier to Marrakech by Tangier–Marrakech Night Express (train)

Trains run frequently from Casablanca to Marrakech. It is a three-hour trip and the cost is nominal.

GETTING AROUND

Buses are widely available and cheap. The bus stations are centrally located in the heart of Marrakesh. They offer routes all over Marrakesh and throughout Morocco. These are privately operated buses while Supratours are city buses. https://www.marrakechairporttransfer.com/ctm-bus-station-marrakech/

Taxis are a good option in Marrakesh, so long as you know a few things beforehand. First, there are two types of cabs: Petit and Grand. Always negotiate the price before getting into a Grand Taxi. Always insist on the cabbie starting the meter in a Petit Taxi. Petit taxis are best for getting around Marrakesh, while Grand Taxis are good for day trips and airport transfers.

Horse-drawn carriages are also available. You will find them waiting for tourists all along Jemaa el Fna.

Rental cars are available at the airport.

By foot. Even if you utilize buses and taxis, you will be walking a lot. Wear good walking shoes!

Documentation

Tourist visas are not required for Morocco (except for residents of South Africa) unless you plan to stay for more than ninety days. **Passports** must be valid for six months from the date of entry into the country. Since requirements can always change, it is best to check to make sure you don't need a visa, http://www.moroccanconsulate.com/visa.cfm. You must also show your return ticket or ticket to your next destination. Upon arrival at the airport you should receive a stamp in your passport. Make sure that you get this stamp because it can be hard to leave Morocco without proof of entry. For some reason, the stamps do not get entered on occasion.

An **International Certificate of Vaccination for Yellow Fever** is required if you are coming from an infected area within the last five days.

About Money…

It's best to convert money at the exchange bureaus in the airport for no or low fees. There are some bureaus in the city center, but it is best for convenience sake to exchange at the airport. There are some ATMS and bureaus near the main square, but disreputable people keep an eye on these places and will come up to you after you have completed your transaction and offer to guide you or take you somewhere. Carry only what you think you'll need each day. Don't pull out your money on the street. Have a bit of money (Moroccan Dirhams) handy to pull out if you buy something, but keep the rest secure elsewhere on your person or with your traveling companion. You will need lots of small bills or coins for tipping, which is expected everywhere. Be sure to spend all your dirhams as it is illegal to take the currency out of the country.

FYI: Be advised that Pickpockets are prevalent in Marrakesh and Fez. Keep most of your money and documents in a hotel safe or similar. Wear a money belt and pay attention when walking the streets, especially in crowded places.

Be warned that when taking photos, everyone expects a tip, especially in the Jemaa el Fna. You must ask permission first ("Mumkin nkhod tsowera?", which means *May I take a picture?)* and pay $1 for the photo. Some will haggle for $2 or more, but stand your ground. You need to work out the price before you take the photo.

Don't pick up anything in the stalls unless you want to buy it. The Moroccan attitude is "You touch it, you buy it." You will be pursued if you put it down and walk away. If you are interested, point to the item and ask how much. Say no thank you ("La Shokran") if you don't want the item and walk away.

In Jemaa el Fna, there are snake charmers, jugglers, sword-swallowers, and other performers with live animals, during the day. But things are different at night. It is more laid back with storytellers and a food court. However, it is advisable to hire a local, licensed guide. They should have credentials around their neck or you can arrange a guide in advance through your hotel. If you need a cab, leave the square. You will pay less if you get a block or two away, but be careful you don't stray too far. Always ask the price upfront and confirm that price before you get in vehicle.

GENERAL TIPS FOR TRAVELING IN MOROCCO

Do not use your left hand to do anything socially important, like eat or shake hands. Most Moroccans feel that it's unclean. If you are left-handed, use your best judgement.

The CDC and WHO *recommend* the following vaccines for Morocco: typhoid, hepatitis A, hepatitis B, cholera, rabies, and influenza. Most of these relate to contaminated food or water. There are no required vaccines at this time. https://wwwnc.cdc.gov/travel/destinations/traveler/none/morocco

You should bring Imodium and general antibiotics, such as Cipro, with you on any trip.

Take a credit card that does not charge a foreign transaction fee. Be sure to contact your credit card company before your trip to avoid a fraud alert that will shut down your card.

Moroccan Dirhams (DEE-rahm) are the local currency. You cannot take dirhams out of the country so be sure to use up on your taxi ride to the airport or in the airport gift shop. www.oanda.com.

In this day and age, I recommend travel insurance for most trips. You have to purchase insurance at when you book your trip. You cannot buy it later. Be sure to read the fine print. www.insuremytrip.com

FYI: Morocco was the first nation to officially recognize the United States of America as an independent nation. We still enjoy a good relationship between our governments.

Check with https://travel.state.gov/content/travel/en/international-travel/International-Travel-Country-Information-Pages/Morocco.html for the latest travel warnings and advisories.

Women must be careful to be polite and friendly without appearing to be too friendly. Do not tease, touch, or flirt with men of any age. You should be careful not to stare at or even smile at a man as it may be perceived as a come on.

Fast Facts

Size: Marrakesh is 89 square miles and Morocco is 172,410 square miles (about the size of California)

Population: 928,850 (Marrakesh) and 33 million (Morocco).

Currency: Moroccan Dirham. Check out www.oanda.com for currency conversions.

Official Language: Arabic and French

Time Zone: UTC/GMT (+1 hour during Daylight Savings Time)

Nickname: Red City (because of the shade of the walls surrounding Old Town; they were built using red sandstone).

Leading Export: Morocco has many exports, but the top ones are electronic equipment, vehicles, fertilizers, fruits and nuts, clothing, and fish (sardines).

Mint Tea is the national drink and Couscous is the national dish.

Marrakesh is divided into two areas: Old Town (Medina) and Gueliz, which offers modern shops, cafes, and bars.

Soccer is Morocco's most important sport.

The Atlas film studios is considered to be the Hollywood of Morocco. For more than a century, films have been shot here, including blockbusters *Lawrence of Arabia* and *Gladiator*.

Morroco's formal name is *Al Mamlakah al Magribiyah*, or Kingdom of Morocco.

At most country markets throughout Morocco, *sehirras* (witches) dispense potions and curses, as well as advice. This is a common practice. Also, most towns have a local fortune teller (*shuwaf* for male, *shuwaffa* for female) who use cards and other items (crystal balls?) to predict the future— for a price.

Morocco is the only African country that is not a member of the African Union.

The capital of Morocco is Rabat.

Marrakesh is the fifth largest city in Morocco behind Casablanca, Rabat, Fes, and Salé.

Tourism in Morocco is expected to reach 18 million by 2020.

Every neighborhood has a hammam, drinking fountain, mosque, preschool, and communal wood-fired ovens for making couscous. This is the tradition meal on Fridays when families gather after prayers.

National Flag of Morocco

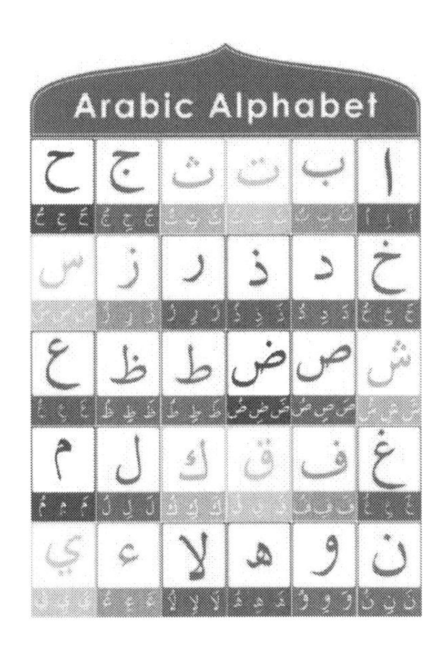

Proper Spelling…

You will see several different ways to spell the same word, such as Marrakech or Marrakesh and Fes or Fez. Both are acceptable spellings. The same is true for Jemaa el Fnaa, which you will also see spelled Djemaa el Fna, as well as many other words. This is due to English and French translations or transliterations of the Arabic word.

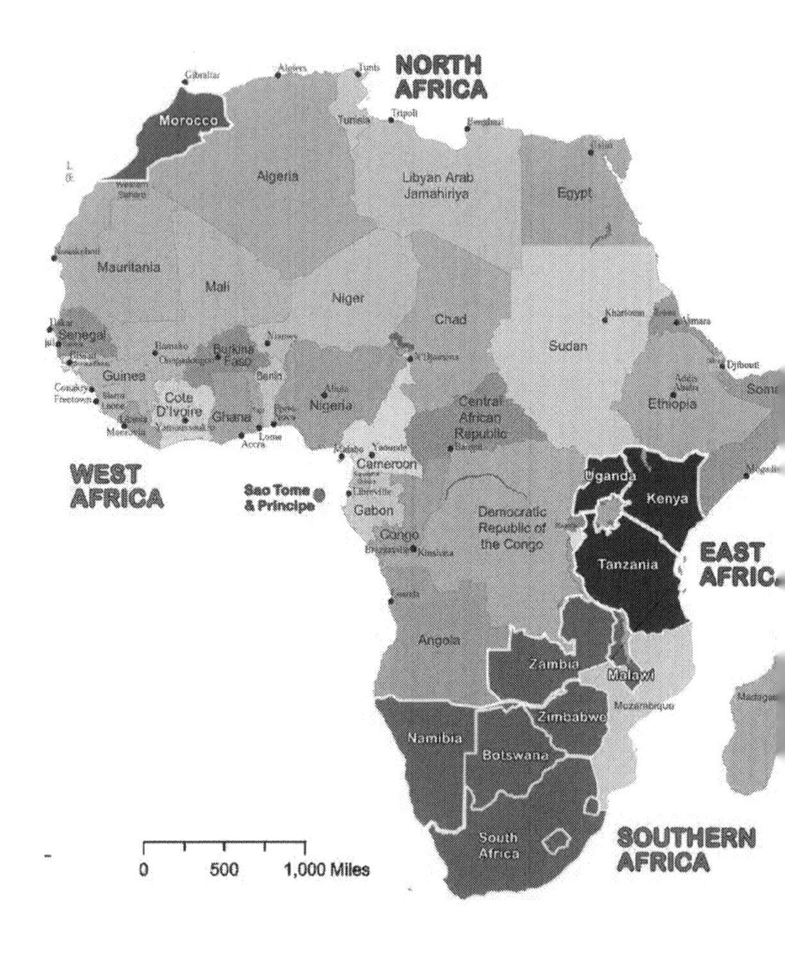

Morocco is located in the northwestern most part of Africa. Morocco borders the North Atlantic Ocean to the west and the Mediterranean Sea to the north, and Algeria, Western Sahara, and Spain as land borders.

TERRANCE'S TOP TEN PICKS

1. **Jemaa el Fna** is the center city shopping mecca, but it is much more. By day, it is a tourist trap of sorts with snake charmers, monkeys, henna ladies (look but don't let them near you), jugglers, and more. Most tourists want to experience this, but I

suggest spending an hour or two during the day doing some shopping and checking out the strange sights and activities, and then returning at night when things are quite different. Most of the

Jemaa el Fna at night reminds me of the German Christmas markets.

performers are gone, as well as the tourists. The square is full of locals and lots of food vendors. The food is good and very reasonably priced. This is a cheap way to try Moroccan cuisine and it feels just like you're at a huge neighborhood barbeque.

Additionally, there are storytellers that will entertain you. Festive and fun!

2. **Camel and Quad Bike Adventure** is a special way to experience this desert region. In the morning, you will journey outside of the city to the edge of the desert and climb aboard your camel to take a ride into a nearby traditional village. You will meet a Moroccan family, sip the national drink

(mint tea), and enjoy some Moroccan snacks and conversation. You will learn about their traditions, customs, and culture. Afterwards, you will bid ado to your camel, enjoy a leisurely Moroccan lunch, and prep for your quad bike adventure. After a brief safety discussion, you will hit the desert. During your exciting excursion, you will see Berber villages and enjoy panoramic views. What a thrilling way to explore and learn! http://www.dunesdeserts.com/.

3. **Atlas Mountains Hot Air Balloon Adventure** offers a lot of fun and some special memories. First, you will be taken from Marrakesh to the flight site where you will enjoy coffee or tea and pastries while watching the balloon being inflated. This is something to see, trust me! Once completed, you will climb aboard and take off for your thrilling ride over the Atlas Mountains at sunrise. I love hot air balloon rides! It is a wonderful experience to soar over dunes, kasbahs, and villages. The baskets hold up to eight passengers and the licensed pilot. Flights usually last 1-2 hours and you will see quite a bit during this time. Also, you will receive a souvenir flight certificate. After disembarking, you enjoy a camel ride and a Berber-style breakfast inside a tent. https://marrakechbyair.com/en/

3. **Take a cooking class**. Foodies will love this option. This small group adventure starts with a guided tour into Jemma el Fna where you'll shop for ingredients. Your guide will explain all about the locally-grown fruits, vegetables, and spices she is selecting for the class. This is a fun and safe way to explore the chaotic Jemaa el Fna. After getting what you need, you will head on to a traditional Moroccan home where you'll start cooking. Typical dishes include couscous

with vegetables, a hearty soup, and some kind of fruit dessert. Moroccan spices and food, such as locally-grown olives, saffron, and citrus fruits will be key ingredients in the dishes you prepare. You will dine al fresco and learn more about Moroccan customs and cuisine. You will meet fellow travelers, locals, and learn so much during this fun, four-hour experience.

http://www.marrakechurbanadventures.com/

Another option: La Maison Arabe was a restaurant that morphed into a hotel and cooking school. Two classes are held each day. During these four-hour classes, students learn how to create Moroccan classics, such as tagine. Every student is assigned his own cooking station complete with homegrown herbs and fresh ingredients. The meals are enjoyed outdoors and you receive a diploma crediting your achievement.

http://www.lamaisonarabe.com/en/ateliers-cuisine.html

5. **Bahia Palace** (pictured here) is situated on nearly twenty acres and boasts more than 150 rooms! It was built for Ahmed Ibn Moussa circa 1895—or rather it was supposedly built to house his many wives and concubines. The most favored women reportedly got the largest bedrooms. Moussa reportedly had four wives and two dozen concubines! Constructed in the classic Moroccan and Islamic style, Bahia Palace boasts amazing architecture. Expert craftsmen were imported from Fes to complete this palace, which took more than fifteen years to build. Bahia Palace literally translates to "palace of the beautiful." And it is with its tile floors, cedar-carved ceilings, marble finishes, and stucco panels. The palatial estate is surrounded by a large, lovely garden. It is among the grandest structures in Marrakesh. At one time, its furnishings were as opulent as the palace itself. Sadly, Moussa's wives and the sultan stripped the

palace of all artwork and furniture upon his death.

http://www.palais-bahia.com/en/

6. **Ourika Valley & Atlas Mountains Adventure**. This full day excursion includes visiting traditional Berber clay villages and learning more about the Berbers. You will also learn all about Moroccan Argan Oil. You will visit a local cooperative where village women made the argan oil, which is one of the best beauty supplements in the world. You will be served Moroccan tea and have a chance to buy these special soaps and oils, if you like. Your journey will include a drive through the Atlas Mountains to Ourika Valley. Upon arrival, you will spend an hour or so trekking and exploring the valley. It is quite scenic with its palm groves and fruit trees. Afterwards, enjoy a leisurely lunch at a riverside restaurant. The highlight of this excursion is a visit to Setti Fatma, which is renowned for its seven waterfalls. Bring your camera! On Mondays, and Thursdays, tours include a visit to a Berber Souk.

https://www.first-marrakech-tours.com/full-day-tour-to-ourika-valley-atlas-mountains.html

FYI: Argan oil is made using the nut of an Argan tree, which only grows in one region of Morocco. The Argan forest has been designated a UNEXCO site to give it protect this important resource. Berber women, working in local cooperatives, hand crack the nuts between two stones. This is a centuries old technique. The raw kernels are extracted from the shell in a stone grinder, hand-kneaded for hours, and finally, cold-pressed

into oil. As if all of that is not enough to merit its value, it takes three days to get four cups of oil! What's more, the oil is loaded with antioxidants, minerals, and fatty acids, including Vitamins A and E. It is a great product because it has many useful purposes: bath oil, moisturizer, toner, soften and condition nail cuticles, hair styling product, hair shampoo and conditioner, and for cooking.

Berber women making Argan oil

7. **Take a private night tour of Marrakesh**. This is an exciting way to explore this city, under the spell of the desert moon and millions of brilliant stars. Marrakesh is a vibrant, bustling place at night. I like it better than during the

daytime. This tour offers participants a safe, fun, and unique way to explore Marrakesh. During this three-hour city tour, you will hear fascinating stories, sample snacks (including Tanjia), explore the city, and experience Jemaa el Fna at night. This square features a huge open-air kitchen with too many food stalls to count, but the guides know the best places. Each vendor features specialties of this region. Also, the guide will show you the seven turns that take you from the heart of the square to quiet, cobblestone streets where most tourists never go. While meandering along these narrow streets, you will learn about local history and see amazing architecture. You will learn intriguing trivia, such as why there has to be two doorways. The evening comes to a close at a rooftop bar where you will enjoy a complimentary, non-alcoholic drink, and hear traditional Moroccan music. If you're not ready to call it a night, your guide will reveal the best places for nightlife or a late night supper.

https://www.withlocals.com/experience/the-magic-of-marrakech-by-night-tour-5fc4a432/

FYI: You may have noticed that most of my TOP TEN picks are guided tours. That is because I think it is safer and easier in Marrakesh to be on a guided expedition. Tourists are heavily targeted and harassed when on their own. Guided tours and day trips protect you from having a negative experience.

8. **Dinner & Chez Ali Equestrian & Moroccan Music Show (Fantasia).** This is a one of a kind and must see event! I'm not even sure I can describe it to you. There is a spectacular opening to this show, which takes place in a huge arena. There are famous folklore groups performing traditional songs and dances, jugglers, belly dancers, a magic flying carpet, acrobats, Arabian horse jumping, a parade, fireworks, and more! Choose from four different menu options at Chez Ali ($-$$$). http://restaurant-chez-ali.com/en/

9. **Stay in a Riad**. There are more than 1,000 riads in Marrakesh. Learn why you need to stay in one for your Moroccan experience to be complete—and authentic. This is discussed in depth in the About Accommodations' chapter.

10. **Get naked at a Moroccan Hamman.** Hammans are an important part of Moroccan culture—right up there with Moroccan tea. Basically, they are Turkish baths (a cleansing

and relaxing treatment that involves spending time in a room filled with steam, followed by washing and massage). Most men, women, and children go on a weekly basis to participate in this cleansing ritual and also to socialize. Men and women are segregated with children going with the appropriate gender. This is one of the rare places where Islam allows women to get naked publicly. Normally, they are required to be clothed from head to toe. If you're shy, you can wear a bathing suit or ask for paper underwear. The ritual lasts about two hours and involves several steps, including prepping, body scrubbing (emphasize the word "scrub") using a special black soap, rinsing, and massage (optional). You will not be touched in any private areas, but you will receive a thorough cleansing otherwise. Moroccans linger in the lounge areas visiting with friends and neighbors.

For a deluxe hammam experience, go to **La Mamounia**. For a more reasonably-priced hammam, try **Hammam de La Rose, Le Bain Bleu**, and **Jardins Mandaline**. It you want a more authentic experience, the locals go to **Hammam Dar el Bacha**. This is the biggest and most traditional hammam in Marrakesh.

FYI: The national animal of Morocco is the Barbary Lion.

Moroccan Recipes

Moroccan Mint Tea

There is no food or drink that is more fundamentally Moroccan than its mint tea. It is served on almost any occasion, such as at breakfast, afternoon tea time, whenever guests are entertained, at business meetings, and whenever a heavy meal (grilled meat or stew) is consumed because it is believed that mint tea helps aid in digestion. We were served pots of it while at a carpet souk, presumably to encourage sales. You will almost assuredly be served mint tea upon arrival at your hotel or riad. Fekkas (a sweet cracker) or some other "dwaz atay" may accompany it. The tea is usually served on silver trays and in silver teapots with ornate glasses, sprigs of Moroccan mint, and lots of sugar.

INGREDIENTS (Makes 6-8 glasses):

1 tablespoon loose gunpowder green tea

3-4 tablespoons granulated sugar

3 1/2 cups water

1/2 cup fresh mint leaves

Tea glasses (not tea mugs)

Tea kettle

Teapot

Heat the water in your tea kettle until boiling. Place one tablespoon of loose tea in your teapot. When water has come to full boil, pour ½ cup water into teapot. Let stand. After a few minutes, the tea pellets will open. Once this occurs, pour out the water. That's right! I said empty out the water. This unusual step is about "washing" the tea. Some Moroccans go so far as to complete a second "washing." That is up to you but I don't believe it's necessary. Add the rest of the water to the teapot and then add the sugar. Put the teapot on the burner with the lid open. Bring the tea to a boil once again. When it boils, remove the teapot, add the mint to the pot or the glasses and let sit for 1-2 minutes.

THIS IS VERY IMPORTANT! Do not stir the tea leaves, water, and sugar mixture. This is believed to bruise the delicate leaves, thereby negatively affecting the flavor. Instead, pour the tea from the pot to the glass a few times until you feel it is well mixed. Just as a martini connoisseur will say "Shaken, not stirred!" a Moroccan believes "Poured, not stirred!"

ANOTHER IMPORTANT STEP! Pour the tea close to the glass and raise the teapot slowly and straight up as you pour. Keep lowering and raising the teapot to create more bubbles, which is a key component of Moroccan Mint Tea.

Do not fill glasses more than half full so that there is a cool part of the glass to touch. If you fill the glass too full, it is too hot to the touch.

Some things you may be wondering...

Where do I find gunpowder green tea? Asian markets carry the tea, some grocery stores stock it, and it is available on Amazon. Check on the ethnic aisle of your store, not on the tea aisle. Gunpowder refers to how the tea leaves are processed. They are steamed and rolled into pellets, which unfold in hot water.

Do I need a Moroccan teapot or will any teapot do? Are tea glasses necessary or can I use mugs?

You won't get the bubble effect if you use mugs and a regular teapot. But you don't have to use glasses or a Moroccan teapot.

Do I need to use fresh mint or can I skip this step?

No! This is a key step in the process. It is not mint tea without mint! You can find fresh mint in the grocery stores and it is available in Amazon's grocery store. You may also grow it yourself. It is easy and cheap to grow. You can use less sugar or a sugar substitute.

Health Benefits:

*Settles upset stomach
*Increases focus and alertness
*Decreases anxiety
*Relieves cough and congestion
*Improves Bad Breath

Moroccan Chicken with Preserved Lemon and Olives

Chicken with preserved lemons and olives is a classic Moroccan dish. It is flavorful and delicious! To make stovetop, use a Dutch oven or thick pot. Or you can slow roast in the oven or cook in a tagine. Preserved lemons take a month to cure. Fresh lemons cannot be substituted for preserved lemons, which are available in ethnic grocery stores and on Amazon. Despite what some recipes say, the chicken should be marinated.

Ingredients:

1 whole chicken, skin on or removed, cut into pieces

1/3 cup vegetable oil (or a blend of vegetable oil and olive oil)

2 large yellow onions (1 lb. or 1/2 kg), sliced as thinly as possible

One small handful of fresh cilantro, chopped

One small handful of fresh parsley, chopped

2 or 3 cloves of garlic, finely chopped or pressed

2 teaspoons ginger

1 teaspoon pepper

1 teaspoon turmeric

1/2 teaspoon salt

1/2 teaspoon saffron (crumbled; optional)

Sauce:

1 handful green or red olives, or mixed

1 preserved lemon, quartered and seeds removed

Tsp of butter (optional)

1. Combine the chicken with the onion, garlic, herbs, and spices. Cover and leave the chicken to marinate in the refrigerator overnight or at least for a few hours.

2. Transfer the chicken and onions to your pot or pan. Cover and cook the chicken over medium-low heat for fifteen minutes or until chicken is fall off the bone tender. Stir and turn chicken periodically. This will take 45-55 minutes. Add a little bit of water if chicken seems to need it. When done, transfer the chicken to a plate and keep covered.

3. Continue to cook the sauce over medium-low heat, stirring it from time to time. Add the preserved lemons and olives to the sauce, which should be less sauce and more onions by now. Place the chicken under the broiler to brown the skin and then return to the pot.

4. Serve the chicken on a serving platter. Pour the onion sauce over the top and along the sides. Garnish the chicken with olives and lemons.

Tfah (Moroccan Apple Dessert)

Ingredients:

6 green (tart) apples sliced into wedges

3 lemons

2 cups sugar

2 cups water

2 tbsp. cinnamon

2-4 tbsp. orange blossom water

Remove the yellow part of the lemon peel and cut it into small strips. Juice the lemons, saving ½ up for later. Peel, core, and cut the apples into wedges. Place cinnamon, water, and sugar into saucepan and bring to a low boil. Add apples, lemon juice, lemon rind, and orange blossom water. Cook until the apples and lemon rind are tender but not mushy. Serve at room temperature. Can serve in individual dishes or in a casserole-style dish.

NOTE: Since I had never heard of orange blossom water before I found this recipe, I did a quick search to learn where to find it. You can buy it at Walmart, Amazon, and similar retailers. I saw warnings that it is strong so be sure to start with two tablespoons and then taste to see if you want to add anymore.

For those of you who prefer chocolate in your dessert, I found this yummy recipe that I will be trying out ASAP.

Moroccan Chocolate Cake

INGREDIENTS

1/2 c sugar

3 eggs

1/4 c coconut flour

1/4 c almond flour

4 tsp cocoa powder

2 tsp dry buttermilk (or regular dry milk)

1/2 cup vegetable or coconut oil

1/2 cup water

1/2 cup plain Greek yogurt

Preheat oven to 350F.In a bowl whisk together 1/2 cup sugar, 1/2 cup oil and 1/2 cup water. After mixing add 4 tsp cocoa powder and 2 tsp dry buttermilk. Reserve half of the mixture and set aside. To the remaining liquid add 3 eggs and 2 tsp baking powder. Whisk well. Slowly add the coconut flour and almond flour, mixing as you go.

Grease an 8″ round baking pan and pour in mixture. Bake for 30 minutes. Remove from oven, and place on a baking rack to cool.

To Make the Glaze

To the reserved chocolate liquid add 1/2 cup of plain Greek yogurt. Whisk until all of the yogurt has been combined. Poke several small holes into the cake using a skewer, toothpick or other small thin object. Pour the glaze over the top of the cake, adding as much or little as to your liking. Cake can also be dusted with powdered sugar before serving and/or topped with fresh fruit.

TOURISTY THINGS TO SEE & DO

Bab Agnaou (pictured here) was built during the 12th century. It is one of the many gates and ramparts of Marrakesh. It is the entrance to the royal Kasbah of Marrakesh and the Saadian Tombs, El Badi Palace, and El Mansouria.

Bahia Palace is still used by the Moroccan royal family of King Mohammed VI on occasion. Their quarters are not part of the palace that is open to the public. The twenty-acre estate is comprised of many buildings, courtyards, gardens, stables, orchards, a school, mosque, and the palace. The palace itself consists of many salons, rooms, and apartments. Today, the palace is open to visitors, art exhibitions, and concerts. http://www.palais-bahia.com/en/

Ben Youssef Madrassa was once the biggest and best Islamic school in the country. The college had 130 rooms and served close to 1,000 students. It is considered to be a key historic site.

Berber Museum houses an impressive collection of historical objects. The 600+ artifacts and artworks are exhibited in the former painting studio of Jacque Majorelle. The history of the Berbers is worth knowing considering that this North Africa tribe date back to the earliest recordings in history. Although once a majority, the Berbers are now a minority population. The exhibits include ceremonial objects, weapons, costumes, musical instruments, carvings, carpets, elaborately decorated doors, and more. Outside the museum is a botanical garden boasting hundreds of different species of plants. This is a good place to go to get a quick overview of the history of this region and to see examples of centuries of Moroccan artwork and artifacts in one place. https://visitmarrakech.com/discover-marrakech/tourist-attractions/berber-museum

Dar Si Said Museum, housed in a palace, displays Berber and Moorish jewelry, ceremonial costumes, weapons, carpets, carvings, decorated doors, and artwork.

Dar Tiskiwin is one of the oldest museums in Marrakesh. Its collection of North African art and artifacts were collected by its founder, Bert Flint, and housed in his former riad. Flint was a Dutch anthropologist.

Djemaa el Fna (Jemaa el Fna) is the heart and soul of Marrakesh. A visit to this square is a must for tourists. Filled with food and crafts stalls, the square is bustling day and night. There are performers during the day, such as snake charmers, magicians, and acrobats. In the evenings, they are replaced with storytellers and musicians. While there is crime in every city around the world, the authorities here work hard to protect tourists visiting the square. Be careful of pickpockets and when taking photographs. Vendors and entertainers expect compensation if you take a photo of them. If you hire a guide to help you explore the square or the city, be sure it is a licensed guide.

El Badi Palace is a historic ruins, but when it was built in the 16th century, it was a spectacular place. It took twenty-five years to complete construction. Gold, onyx, and marble were used throughout the palace, which boasts more than 350 rooms and pavilions. It is open to the public.

FYI: The Royal Palace is not open to the public. You will only be able to see a guard gate, walls, and palm trees. You are not even permitted to take photos! The guards will chase you off if you try.

Gueliz is the new part of Marrakesh. It has a large residential and commercial area that includes lots of shops, cafes, and restaurants. Its main streets are Avenue Mohammed V and Avenue Mohammed VI.

Look for the bright blue exterior and the strange looking entrance door!

Jardin Majorelle is a twelve-acre botanical garden filled with cacti, fruit trees, exotic plants, and many species of birds. Created by French painter Jacques Majorelle, this exquisite garden is one of the most visited places in Morocco. The

gardens surround the **Majorelle Museum**, which houses Islamic art.
http://jardinmajorelle.com/ang/

Koutoubia Mosque is the largest mosque in Marrakesh. Dating back to 1150, the most notable feature is its minaret, which is topped with four copper balls (also called globes) of various sizes. The 230-foot tower can be seen from almost anywhere in the city. The tower contains six rooms “stacked” one on top of the other. This design was so that no one could glimpse the king’s harem. The prayer hall holds more than 25,000 worshippers. Non-Muslims may not enter this holy site.

Koutoubia Gardens (pictured here) are located behind the mosque. While non-Muslims cannot enter the mosque, they are welcome in the gardens. Free and open to the public, the gardens are full of exotic flowers, beautiful roses, enormous palm trees, and fruit trees.

La Mamounia is one of the best hotels in Marrakesh. It is included in this list of tourist attractions because of its historical significance. The gardens were given to Prince Al Mamoun by his father as a wedding gift. The hotel was built around the gardens. It opened its doors in 1923. It is a blend of Arabic-Andalusian architecture, which has been appreciated by many famous folks over the years. The list includes Actor Charlie Chaplin, Musician Ray Charles, Fashion designer Yves Saint-Laurent, the Beatles, Elton John, Charles De Gaulle, and Winston Churchill. The Moroccan palace hotel features four restaurants, gardens, spa, boutique, superior rooms, suites, riads, and amazing artwork. https://www.mamounia.com/en/

La Maison de la Photographie is a photography museum founded by two collectors of vintage Moroccan photography. The gallery contains thousands of photographs, glass negatives, and documents related to photography in Morocco.

FYI: If you buy a "hop on, hop off" bus pass, it includes stops at all the major tourist attractions, which are too spread out to explore by foot. The pass allows visitors to "hop on and hop off as they please. Tourists can purchase a one-day pass or a multi-day pass.

The buses are double decker so you can sit inside or out in the open. Also, the buses are 100% electric so they are environmentally friendly.

Choose the Historic (18 stops including Bahia Palace and Jemaa el Fna) or Palm Grove (13 stops in northern area of city) route.

https://www.viator.com/tours/Marrakech/Marrakech-City-Tour-Hop-On-Hop-Off/d5408-70964P1

Mellah (Jewish Quarter) was once home to more than 250,000 Jews. Today, there are far fewer Jews and the neighborhood has deteriorated. Nonetheless, it is worth visiting. You may wish to hire a local guide to take you around the Mellah.

Menora Gardens are at the gates of the Atlas Mountains. There is an artificial lake, orchards, and a pavilion. This park is perfect for picnicking. There is a nearby stream and according to legend, its waters bring "good luck" or "Baraka", so it is a popular place. The original gardens date back to the 12th century, but the current pavilion was built during the 19th century by the Sultan for his family. The gardens are free and open to the public.

Marrakech Museum is housed in the Dar M'Nebhi Palace. This museum boasts an excellent collection of Berber, Muslim, and Jewish art and artifacts. The items are displayed in dozens of different rooms. The palace museum has a large covered courtyard, pillars, passageways, and decorated windows and doors. Be sure to look up to admire the huge chandelier.

Marrakech Medina is a UNESCO World Heritage Site. It is full of historical monuments, mosques, tombs, and palaces. It was built in the 11th century by the Almoravids.

Museum of African Contemporary Art Al Maaden (MACAAL) is a private Moroccan art collection, amassed over the last forty years or so, forms the museum's permanent collection of some 2,000 contemporary works and educational programs are offered. Admission is free.

Ramparts are the protective walls that surround the city. Much of the twelve miles of ramparts still exist. Marrakesh is nicknamed "Red City" because of the reddish pink sandstone used to build these walls. Some of the elaborate gates or "babs" still stand. The Bab Agnaou is the entrance to the Kasbah. It is probably the most impressive rampart that still exists. Visitors can walk around the ramparts or hire a horse-drawn carriage and ride around it.

Saadian Tombs can be found just outside the city proper. Sultan Ahmed el Mansour built the tombs during the 16th century. He was buried here, as well as hundreds of other Saadian dynasty and royal descendants. Loyal servants and soldiers were buried in the gardens. The mausoleums are incredible with domed ceilings and mosaics, as is the cemetery garden.

Saint Martyrs Church was the first church built in Marrakesh. This Catholic Church was built in 1928 under the French Protectorate. It can be found in Gueliz. Mass is held weekdays and Sundays. It is open to the public.

Moroccan Spices

Souks of Marrakesh are the local markets and a must for tourists. There is no better way to experience Moroccan way of life than to explore the souks. Here you can buy just about anything, from spices to cosmetics. There are five main souks and several smaller souks. You may wish to buy a pair of authentic Moroccan leather slippers (babouches). Negotiating is expected. Be sure to counter with a much lower bid than the merchant offers, such as half as much. Marrakech has the largest traditional marketplace in Morocco, and the souks can be a confusing labyrinth and a bit intimidating for first-time visitors. You may wish to hire a guide. If not, you will probably get lost, but will eventually find your way out. Some vendors are very polite and some can be aggressive. They may follow you around trying to convince you to come to their store. Be polite but firm when you are not interested, clearly stating you are not interested, and move on (and ignore them) and they will usually get the hint. Some vendors will offer you tea, but you better be serious about buying their wares to accept.

Tanneries are where leather is processed in Marrakesh. Morocco is a leading exporter of leather products. Some will swear you have to see the tanneries, but I disagree. I don't see the thrill. If you are going to Fes, there are better tanneries there. If you're not going to Fes and you have your heart set on seeing the tannery vats, the Bab Debbagh Tannerie is one of the most popular tanneries. As soon as you get to the gate, a guide will be waiting. You will be given mint twigs to help mask the awful smell of the tanneries. These guides will expect a large sum of money from you after your tannery tour. If you don't want a guide, be clear you will not pay for their services.

Tin Mal Mosque is one of the only mosques in Marrakesh that allows non-Muslims inside. It was built by Mohammad Tumart. The ceilings are cedar carved and the long archways are amazing. There is no entrance fee, but tourists are expected to tip the guard.

Marrakech's Palm Grove (Palmeraie) has over 100,000 palm trees and is a great place to enjoy some quiet time.

FYI: Decorated doors are an important part of Moroccan architecture. They are made of cedar, camel bone, metal, plaster, and wrought iron. They are adorned with motifs, bright paint, and ornate door knockers. You will notice the Hand of Fatima on many doors, which is a protectorate against the Evil Eye.

ADVENTURE ACTIVITIES & DAY TRIPS

There are many adventurous options for travelers, such as cultural dinner shows, quad biking, trekking, camel rides, ballooning, rafting, jet skiing, skiing, surfing, wakeboarding, rock climbing, canyoning, horseback riding, snowboarding, tuk tuk tours, kayaking, shopping, cooking classes, specialty tours, helicopter rides, and more. http://www.rafting.ma/ and https://www.viator.com/Marrakech/d5408-ttd

Here are a few fun possibilities:

Day Trip to the **Atlas Mountains, Berber Villages, & Spectacular Imlil & Toubkal Valley**.
https://www.atlastrekshop.com/day-walk-marrakech-atlas.html

Day Trip to **Essaouira**, which is a beautiful old Portuguese town. There is a lovely beach, pretty port, sakal, and souks.

https://www.atlastrekshop.com/1-day-essaouirra-trip.html

Thirty-minute Helicopter Sightseeing Ride over Marrakesh and High Atlas Mountains. Or, go for a Sahara Desert Safari. A helicopter will take you from Marrakesh to Sahara. Upon arrival, you will enjoy a camel ride and then spend the night in a luxury Berber Desert Camp in the Sahara Desert. You will be served a delicious dinner and be entertained with music afterwards. You will watch the sunrise and then enjoy a big breakfast before your return flight to Marrakesh.
http://www.moroccoactiveadventure.com/helicopter-tours/

Sahara Desert Adventure includes a visit to Ouarzazate, known as the "Hollywood of Morocco" where many famous movies have been made (such as *Star Wars, The Mummy, Gladiator*, *Cleopatra, Game of Thrones*, *Sahara*, and *Lawrence of Arabia*). This adventure includes a tour of locations, lot of movie trivia, a

lovely desert dinner & bonfire, short hike, camel ride, overnight camping, and exploring an ancient Kasbah.
http://berberadventures.com/sahara.htm

Camel Ride, Quad Biking, and Spa Treatment Day Adventure. Enjoy a leisurely camel ride through the famed Palm Grove, followed by an exhilarating quad bike ride, tea with a Moroccan family, and finish the day with a Hammam spa experience.
https://www.clickexcursions.co.uk/

FYI: Atlas Mountains are 25 miles from Marrakesh. Essaouria and Ouarzazate/Ait Ben Haddou Kasbah (UNESCO World Heritage Site) are 120 miles from Marrakesh.

FIVE MORE PLACES IN MOROCCO WORTH VISITING…

Menknes: Located in northern Morocco, Meknes is small, but has lots to offer. This former capital city has a 9th-century medina, Mausoleum of Moulay Ismail, Bab Mansour, Dar Jamai Museum, and famous Roman ruins (pictured here), Volubilis.

Fes (or Fez): Also a former capital city, Fes is a popular tourist destination due to its tanneries (pictured here), Merenid Tombs, Dar el-Makhzen, Mellah, and large medina, which is a UNESCO World Heritage Site.

Tangier (pictured here) is the quintessential north African town and gateway to Morocco for many travelers arriving via the Strait of Gilbraltar. Many American writers frequented Tangier during the 1940s-60s, such as Truman Capote and Tennessee Williams. Visits to the Kasbah, Kasbah Museum, medina, Jewish cemetery, Cap Spartel Lighthouse, and Ville Nouvelle are a must. Tangier is the oldest city in Morocco.

Dades Valley (pictured here) lies between Jebel Sarhro and the High Atlas Mountains. For those seeking to connect with nature, this is the place to do it. The best way to explore is on foot through Berber villages, Dades Gorges, Todra, and former forts (kasbahs), which have been converted into hotels.

Jebel Toubkal (pictured here) is the place for those seeking extreme adventure. It is the highest peak in North Africa. At 13,667 feet, the trek to the snow-covered summit atop the High Atlas Mountains is no easy feat. However, you can summit it and return in one day, but two is recommended for optimal acclimatization. Be

sure to stop in Imlil on your way back. Imlil is a small, mountain village that is 5,900-feet above sea level and located at the base of Jebel Toubkal. Its economy relies chiefly on agriculture and tourism. The movie, *Seven Years in Tibet* (Brad Pitt), was filmed here. There was a huge flood in 1995 that killed 150 people, including 60 tourists.
https://www.tourdust.com/blog/posts/atlas-mountains and
http://www.naturallymorocco.co.uk/

BEST OF MARRAKESH

BEST HIPSTER RESTAURANT: Nomad is close to Jemaa el Fna. It is a multi-level restaurant that is super cool and contemporary. Features Moroccan cuisine with a twist. Hip cocktails, such as cucumber martinis and mojitos, are served.
http://www.nomadmarrakech.com/

BEST COCKTAILS: Nomad is one of the few places in Marrakesh that serves alcoholic beverages and does it well. Their rooftop terrace is a great spot to enjoy a cold beverage.
http://www.nomadmarrakech.com/

BEST FINE DINING: Le Grande Table Marocaine can't be beat. Your experience begins with orange blossom water brought to your table to cleanse your hands. Regional cuisine is served, including a seafood tagine and gnocchi spiced with saffron. A musician plays an oud (Arabic string instrument) in the open-air courtyard. It is expensive, so be warned.

https://www.royalmansour.com/

BEST BUDGET DINING: You can't beat the stalls at **Jemaa el Fna** for great food at low price, but it is more enjoyable at night.

BEST PLACE TO EAT TO GIVE BACK TO COMMUNITY: **Amal Centre** is part of an initiative to help women, so it is staffed by all women who prepare delicious, home cooked Moroccan meals. Their food is so sought after that reservations are required. Eat here and you not only get a delicious breakfast or lunch, you are empowering women. You may take a cooking (learn how to make couscous, a tajine, or pastilla) or baking class (Moroccan pastries) at the center. http://amalnonprofit.org/

BEST CREPES: La Creperie serves the best crepes I've ever had. You have got to try their chicken, peppers, onions, and cheese crepe. Yum! They also serve vegetarian and dessert crepes.
https://www.facebook.com/creperiedemarrakech/

BEST DESERT ADVENTURE: Hot-air ballooning over the High Atlas Mountains. There is no better view of Marrakesh and mountains. This once-in-a-lifetime experience begins at sunrise. You will drink coffee and eat pastries as you watch your balloon being inflated. After your incredible flight, you will enjoy a full Berber breakfast and then a desert camel ride.
https://www.onthegotours.com/us/Morocco/Best-Places-To-Visit/Marrakech/Atlas-Mountains-Hot-Air-Balloon-Ride

BEST THRILL: Outside of Marrakesh is a place most tourists never discover. **Terres d'Amanar** is a 173-acre adult playground complete with mountain biking, trail running, climbing, archery, trekking, zip lining, swimming, horseback riding, and more.
http://www.terresdamanar.com/

FYI: A tagine is the distinctive Moroccan cooking dish with a funnel shaped lid. It's also the name of the slow-cooked meal cooked within the clay pot. Tagines come in many varieties, including chicken, lamb, beef, and vegetarian, and with many varieties of flavors. One traditional recipe mixes lemons preserved in salt, chicken and olives to result in delicious citrus flavored dish. Another classic recipe is made from lamb and dried figs.

BEST WALKING TOUR OF MARRAKESH: Accompanied by a licensed guide, you'll navigate Marrakech's chaotic medina and its colorful souks. The three-hour tour includes all of the city's important historic sites and Jemaa el Fna. It also includes pick up and drop off, A/C vehicle, entrance fees, and (6) languages are available, including English and Spanish. **Get Your Guide** offers other great tours too. www.getyourguide.com
RUNNER UP: MARRACH CITY BIKE TOUR is a great way to get around and drinks are included. You will see all the major attractions during this 3-hour tour. https://www.viator.com/tours/Marrakech/Marrakech-City-Bike-Tour/d5408-9144P1?SSAID=865381&aid=sas0_132440_865381&mcid=43009&SSAIDDATA=SSCID%5F71k2%5F7rhxr

BEST FAMILY RESTAURANT: Exotic Bali is a great place to go with kids or just adults who are tired of Moroccan food. The ambience is fun and laid back. They serve Asian and Indonesian food, including soups, appetizers, entrees, and desserts. Reasonably-priced and great service. http://exotic-bali.com/

BEST FOOD TOUR: Foodies will love **Marrakech Food Tours**. Sample Moroccan dishes you won't discover on your own, which focus on traditional home-cooked Moroccan foods. Led by a lovely husband and wife team, you will eat olives from the local market, msemmen chema (pan-fried dough), khobz bread, lamb prepared in two different ways (mechoui and tangia), sheep's head (for the adventurous eaters), traditional Moroccan vegetable couscous, sweet mint tea, cookies, fruit smoothies, and more. https://marrakechfoodtours.com/

FYI: Be sure to drink bottled in Marrakesh and throughout Morocco. Also, Moroccan mint tea and Berber tea are plentiful and will keep you hydrated. Orange juice is made using the sweetest, local oranges. OJ is so refreshing on a hot day.

BEST SPLURGE: Outside of the city is an oasis, if you can afford it. **Beldi Country Club** (pictured here) is a perfect respite during your hectic Moroccan adventure. Situated on forty acres, the hotel offers 38 suites that resemble a Moroccan village. There are several gardens (including a beautiful rose garden), huge olive trees, salons, a riad, ksar, courtyards, and solarium. There are shops that sell Moroccan handbags, carpets, cushions, hand-blown glass, and more. There are two hammams on the premises and lots of activities: tennis, swimming (three pools), golf, pottery course, cooking lessons, bread making lessons, movies, quad, horseback riding, and a French game, Petanque Strip. http://beldicountryclub.com/en/hotel

BEST ROOFTOP BAR: Kechmara is a fun place to grab a drink in Gueliz and see the town from its spacious, yet cozy, roof terrace. There is an impressive cocktail menu and lots of yummy food.
http://www.kechmara.com/Kechmara_Bar_Restaurant_Marrakech.html

BEST HASSLE FREE SHOPPING: Ensemble Arisanal is Marrakesh's version of a department store. It only sells handicrafts, so it is a great place for tourists to find souvenirs without having to endure the haggling and chaos of the medina. The store sells jewelry, carpets, kaftans, jellabas, babouches, embroidery, handbags, and more. Avenue Mohammed V, Gueliz.

BEST TRADITIONAL HAMMAM: El Basha (Dar El Bacha) is the oldest and biggest hammam in Marrakesh. It is a traditional hammam with attendants and separate areas for men and women. It also has different times with men coming in the morning and women in the afternoons and evenings. Street 20 Rue Fatima Zohra.

BEST DELUXE HAMMAM: La Mamounia can't be beat. In addition to many treatment options, such as sugar rose body wrap, argan oil massage, facials, sculpting, and hot stone massages, La Mamounia has a lovely swimming pool, gym facilities, and French or Italian restaurants. Make a day of it! https://www.mamounia.com/en/hotel-spa-marrakesh/spa-hammam.html

BEST HAMMAM FOR COUPLES: Les Bains de Marrakech is one of the few hammams that offer joint massage and hammam rooms. They have a swimming pool, courtyard, lounge area, bathing areas, and treatment rooms. Reserve a space as soon as possible as it books up. Be sure to try their mud wrap with essential oils. http://www.lesbainsdemarrakech.com/en/home

BEST BRUNCH: **Crystal** serves brunch every weekend from noon – 4 p.m. The ambience is soothing and upbeat with jazz music and live acapella performances. International dishes, patisseries, and cocktails are served. http://www.pachamarrakech.com/en/crystal-restaurant.htm

BEST BAKERY: Rouge Vanille serves delicious pastries, cakes, brunch, and more—and they're cheap. https://www.facebook.com/rougevanille

BEST PLACE FOR COFFEE: Café de France in Gueliz serves excellent coffee and fresh squeezed orange juice. http://www.cafe-france-marrakech.com/

FYI: There is a Starbucks in in Carre Eden shopping center in Gueliz.

BEST PLACE FOR TEA: Tchaba Tea House was founded in the United Arab Emirates, but has expanded into Dubai, Abu Dhabi, and Marrakesh. They sell fifty different designer teas and the way they serve it as something to see and experience. Avenue Mohammed VI, Gueliz.

BEST PLACE FOR AMERICAN FOOD: The Sandwich Factory serves all American sandwiches and hot dogs, if your stomach needs a break from spicy food. https://www.facebook.com/TheSandwichFactoryMarrakech/

BEST VEGETARIAN: La Famille serves great vegetarian meals and desserts. Their service and laid back atmosphere is perfect. https://www.facebook.com/La-famille-marrakech/

FYI: If you'd like to try a local delicacy, Café Clock serves the best camel burgers in town. It is best to avoid fried fish and ground beef in Marrakesh. Grilled foods are the safest bets. Also, watch where the locals go, especially in Jemaa el Fna. That's where you want to eat.

About Islam…

Morocco is one of the most liberal Muslim countries. Nonetheless, it is a conservative culture and you need to understand and respect the religion while in this country.

You will hear the call to prayer ring throughout the city five times a day. Muslims are expected to go to holy sites to pray during these times. Non-Muslims are not allowed inside these mosques, but are permitted on the grounds. Friday is the Muslim day of congregational prayer, so some businesses and restaurants are closed. Public displays of affection are frowned upon, public intoxication is a no no, offering alcohol to a Muslim is a no no, and you should definitely dress conservatively (see 'How to Pack' for more information).

Their holy book is the Koran, which is based on the teachings of the Prophet Mohammed. Each Muslim practices the five tenets, called the Pillars of Islam. These require that the faithful profess their faith, pray five times a day, practice charity, fast during Ramadan, and make a pilgrimage to Mecca.

If you visit during the month of Ramadan when the faithful fast each day from sun up until sunset, you will have a slightly different experience than a visit at other times of the year. However, you won't be expected to fast, and there will be restaurants open in Marrakesh. We visited Morocco during Ramadan and the biggest thing was that it was less crowded during the day and also a siren sounded nightly that signaled the end of the day's fasting.

ABOUT ACCOMMODATIONS

Lodging options are plentiful in Marrakesh. Visitors can choose from hotels (budget to luxury), riads, and hostels. Like lodging anywhere in the world, all of these vary greatly from one to five stars. I highly recommend you stay in a riad, if you want an authentic Moroccan experience. In fact, that's the focus of this list. To put it simply, a riad is a wonderful combination of guest house, bed and breakfast inn, and boutique hotel. But you can find more lodging options on www.airbnb.com, www.booking.com, and www.hotels.com.

BEST MODERATELY-PRICED RIAD: **Dar Hanane** is centrally located in the Marrakesh Medina. It has a rooftop terrace, open fireplace salon, and patio. http://www.dar-hanane.com/

BEST BUDGET RIAD: Centrally-located **Riad Yasmine** has eight lovely guest rooms. Free Wi-Fi is included and other amenities include A/C, private patio, lounge area, flat screen television, roof top solarium, pool, library (books and games), restaurant, and laundry service. Plus, continental breakfast is included. https://www.riad-yasmine.com/

BEST RATED: Riad Signature is centrally-located near Jemaa el Fna. It features a dining room with fireplace, living room/lounge, patio with fountain, hammam, and terrace with pool and solarium. http://www.riad-signature.com/

BEST OVERALL: Riad Warda is less than five minutes from Jemaa el Fna. It has an indoor court with fountain, living room, mezzanine, A/C, private baths, rooftop terrace, free Wi-Fi, television with international channels, and free local calls. https://www.riadwarda.com/

BEST FAMILY: Riad Dar Nakous, centrally-located, offers both junior suites and family rooms. They offer kids meals, kids entertainment, strollers, babysitting, bike rentals, swimming pool, BBQ facilities, free laundry service, shuttle service and airport drop off ($),

and concierge service.
http://riaddarnakous.riad.website/en/

BEST LUXURY: Palais Riad Lamrani features a lovely garden, rooftop terrace, hammam, restaurant and lounge/bar with grand piano, swimming pool, and luxury rooms and suites. http://www.palaislamrani.com/en/
RUNNER UP: El Fenn, https://el-fenn.com/

BEST INTERACTIVE: Dar Anika can't be beat. The owners will accompany you on your trip to the nearby medina, offer advice on things to do and where to eat, spa treatments, hammam, and cooking classes are given. There is a pool and restaurant on site. Free Wi-Fi and breakfast is included. http://riadanika.com/

BEST POOL/LOUNGE AREA: Riad Malika has the best swimming pool, bar, and lounging area. It is the oldest riad and has the most character, in my opinion. Breakfast is serve in the terrace, lunch is served poolside, and dinner

is served in the exotic, candlelit garden.
http://www.riadmalika.com/en/

BEST ROOMS/SUITES: Riad Anabel has lovely guest rooms with private baths, roof terrace, pool, patio, hammam, and spa.
http://www.riadanabel.com/en/

BEST ECO-FRIENDLY: Riad Porte Royale is a lovely place with lots of amenities (Egyptian cotton linen and full breakfast), including concierge services. Bio shower gels and shampoos with Argan oil and triple-filtered water (eliminates plastic bottles) are just some of the ways they are reducing their carbon footprint.
http://www.riadporteroyale.com/

BEST HOSTELS: Young and Happy Hostel, Dream Kasbah, Hostel Waka Waka (pictured here)**, Hostel Marrakech Rouge, Hostel Kif Kif,** and **Kaktus Hostel**. These are all comparable in price—most are $5-$10 a night!) with basic dorm rooms and private rooms. These can all be booked using www.booking.com or www.hostelworld.com. Most are very clean, centrally-located, and include free Wi-Fi and breakfast.

BEST BUDGET HOTEL: Les Trois Palmiers offers free Wi-Fi, buffet breakfast, pool, airport transportation, and restaurant. It is at the train station, not near the medina. http://lestroispalmiers.com/

BEST LUXURY HOTEL: Royal Mansour Marrakech was commissioned King Mohammed VI. In addition to being well-known for guest privacy, amenities are among the best in the world. There is a tea lounge, spa gardens, three Michelin-star restaurants, cigar bar, lounge, and private guest riads. Guests will be awed by the carved cedar wood, stained glass, suede and silk carpets, velvet brocade sofas and chandeliers from Lalique, Baccarat and Venice. https://www.royalmansour.com/en/a-unique-place/ **RUNNER UP: LA MAMOUNIA,** https://www.mamounia.com/en/

BEST CAMPING: Ourika Camp has a TV room, playground, sauna, aqua gym, restaurant, library, Wi-Fi, and lots of entertainment/activities. http://www.camping321.com/en/campsite/ourika-camp-85119.html

BEST TOUR OPERATORS:

www.adventures-abroad.com

www.authentic-morocco.com

www.morocco-travel.com

www.gateway2morocco.com

www.naturallymorocco.co.uk

www.tribes.co.uk

www.zicasso.com

About Scams…

The biggest scam in Marrakesh is fake guides and they are everywhere. Licensed guides have official badges they wear around their necks, so be sure to inspect and only use licensed guides. A plus to hiring a licensed guide is they will keep fake guides and other disreputable folks away from you. Fake guides will try to take you on 'special tannery tours' or tell you they 'work for your hotel' or tell you they can take you to the 'best shop with lowest prices'. The best way to avoid unpleasant encounters is to know where you're going (or at least fake it). Study your map before going outside. Walk purposefully.

Politely shrug off unwanted help. Don't take photos in Jemaa el Fna unless you are willing to pay a tip, which you should negotiate beforehand. Always pay attention to your surroundings and stay in the tourist areas unless you have guide. Expect to haggle when buying just about anything in Marrakesh. This is not a scam, just part of the culture. Walk away if you get tired or uncomfortable with haggling. Be sure to thank the vendor before moving on.

Useful Phrases

Ahlan (Hello or Welcome)

Ma'a salama (Goodbye)

Ana jae'/ ana 'atshaan (I'm hungry/thirsty)

Ayn (Where?)

Yajebu an adhaba al aan! (I have to go now!)

Shokran (Thank You)

Esmee (My name is...)

Ada'tutareeqi (I'm lost)

Hal beemkanekmosa'adati? (Can you help me?)

Bi kam? (How much is this?)

Na'am/Laa (Yes/No)

Ma femtesh (I don't understand)

Aynayaqao al hammam law samaht? (Where are the toilets please?)

Aynaajedosayarata el ojra? (Where can I get a taxi?)

ABOUT MARRAKESH

Sultan Youssef Ibn Tachfin, the first of the Moroccan (Berber) Almoravid dynasty, established Marrakesh in 1062. Ramparts were built around the city's medina to protect it. This twelve-mile, 19-foot high defensive wall was built using sandstone that is a unique shade of pinkish red. The fortification includes 200 square towers and twenty gates. This is how Marrakesh got its nickname, "Red City. Although nicknamed "Red City", Marrakesh means "Land of God."

The Almohade dynasty began in 1147. Abd al Mu'min did not feel the mosques built by the Almoravids were correctly oriented, so he had two new mosques built. Koutoubia Mosque and the Ben Youssef Mosque are two of the best known mosques in the world.

Interestingly, Morocco had the largest Jewish community in the Muslim world. An edict from King Ferdinand II ordered the expulsion of all Jews from Spain in 1492. In 1496, King Manuel I also evicted all Jews from Portugal. Many of these Jews ended up in North Africa's Morocco. They numbered as high as 350,000 at one time, but today the Moroccan Jewish population is less than 3,500 in the Old

Jewish Quarter or mellah. But the city still has the three large synagogues and cemetery that were built for the influx of Moroccan Jews.

The Marinids dynasty took over in 1230 and ruled for more than two centuries before being replaced by the Wattasids dynasty. Next came the Saadians, who were responsible for unifying Morocco. The next, and current, dynasty, is the Alouites.

Until 1867, Europeans were forbidden from entering Marrakesh unless granted permission by the Sultan. But they came anyway. Morocco was conquered by Portugal, Spain, and France. Peace was uncommon in Morocco until the country gained its independence in 1956.

The capital was moved from Marrakesh to Rabat in 1911. In 1912, the Treaty of Fes was signed, which made Morocco a French Protectorate but the sultan remained the ruler.

This relationship between Morocco and France was critical to Morocco's growth. If not for France, Morocco's infrastructure would not be nearly as progressive. This includes the rail system, roads, hydro-electrical installations, and irrigation systems. Educated Moroccans still speak French, as well as Arabic.

The modern quarter of Marrakesh, Gueliz, was completed in 1956, just prior to Morocco's independence. Marrakesh has two main areas: Old Town and New Town. The old town is where the historical buildings are located. The new town of Gueliz is largely commercial and residential, built to accommodate the city's expanding population.

Since the birth of Marrakesh, several Moroccan empires have risen and fallen. The country has been conquered many times over. It has suffered famines and plagues, as well as growth and opulence. But all the while, Marrakesh has never lost its sense of identity. It has, however, clashed with Fez. They have always been rivals, fighting to be better than the other. Fez is considered to be the capital of the north (politically), while Marrakesh is the capital of southern Morocco. Fez is larger, but Marrakesh is more popular with tourists. The capital was moved to Rabat in hopes of ending the rivalry. While it may have helped, it certainly did not end the feuding.

Many tourists complain that Fez is too big and modern. Marrakesh is considered to be more tourist-friendly. Long before backpackers found their way to Marrakesh, it was popular with people like British Prime Minister Winston Churchill, renowned fashion designer Yves Saint Laurent, and famous rock bands, The Rolling Stones and The Beatles.

Today, Marrakesh is the fourth largest city in Morocco due to tourism, agriculture, and minerals mined in the Atlas Mountains.

The Medina of Marrakech is a UNESCO World Heritage site. The Jemaa el Fna is the most famous square in Africa. There are more than 400 hotels in Marrakech, plus hundreds of riads. Also, there are hundreds of cafes and restaurants. And there are dozens of mosques, museums, souks, synagogues, gardens, historic sites, and monuments across the city.

But what Marrakesh is best known for is as a bridge between the past and present. It has preserved its cultural heritage and Islamic integrity and made tourists feel most welcome. In fact, the city recently invested $2 billion in tourism infrastructure.

ANNUAL EVENTS & AVERAGE TEMPS

There are dozens festivals and special events held year round. Here is a list of some of the biggest and best. A comprehensive list can be found at http://www.riads-marrakesh.net/city/events-marrakech/.

Marrakech International Magic Festival (March)

Madjazz Festival Marrakech (May)

Ramadan (May-June)

FYI: Ramadan is the ninth month of the Islamic calendar, and is observed by Muslims worldwide as a month of fasting to commemorate the first revelation of the Quran to Muhammad according to Islamic belief. This annual observance is regarded as one of the Five Pillars of Islam. The month lasts 29–30 days, depending on the year.

Marrakech Art Gardens (April)

Marrakech National Folk Art Festival (July)

Sun Festival (July)

Feast of the Throne (July)

Oasis Festival (September)

International Festival of Salsa (September)

Marrakech Jazz (November)

Independence Day (November)

International Film Festival
Marrakech (December)

Marrakech Grand Prix (January)

Marrakech International Marathon (January)

Dakka Marrakchia Festival (February)

Marrakech Golf Festival (February)

1-54 Marrakech (February)

AVERAGE TEMPS

While Marrakesh is a great year round destination, it has four seasons:

December-February is winter with temperatures averaging in the 60s during the day and dropping into the 40s at night. There is also more rain in the winter than any other time of year. If you're interested in skiing, winter is the only feasible time.

March-May is spring and this is one of the best times to visit. Temperatures average in the 70s and lodging is cheaper than in the winter and summer.

June-August is summer and temperatures are often in the triple digits. It can be dangerously hot, especially between 12-3 p.m. Despite the heat, the city is packed with tourists and lodging prices are at their peak.

September-November is their fall and a great time to visit. Temperatures average in the 70s and tourists are less abundant. Deals can be found on lodging during spring and fall, which is known as the shoulder season.

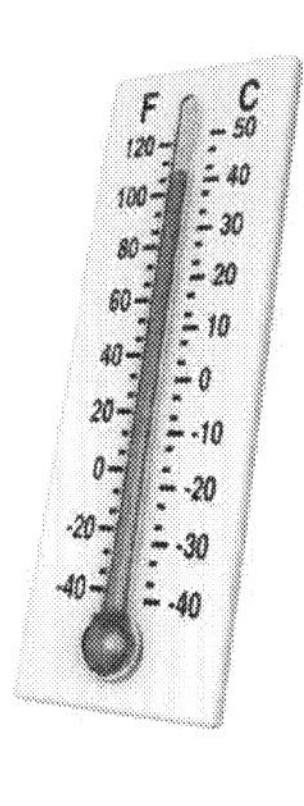

FYI: The highest temperature ever recorded in Marrakesh is 113°F in July. The lowest temperature ever recorded in Marrakesh is 35°F in January.

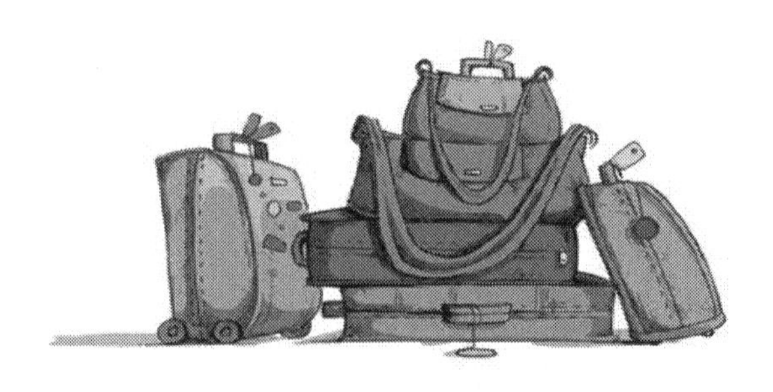

How to Pack

You need to pack conservative clothes because this is a Muslim country. This means no shorts, tank tops, low cut tops, or mini-skirts. Avoid flashy and tight-fitting clothes. Make sure your t-shirts designs aren't controversial or inflammatory. Even though you only need to have your shoulders covered, I show respect by wearing thin ¾ sleeve t-shirts. This also helps protect me from sun damage and insect bites.

I take a backpack rather than a purse. It frees up my hands and is harder for pickpockets to steal. I don't wear any jewelry except a watch, or carry valuables when I go sightseeing. I leave my passport, travel documents, and large sums of cash in a secure place.

If you are staying a week, three or four tops and two pairs of pants should do the trick.

*scarf to cover head when visiting mosques
*walking shoes and high quality socks
*shower shoes/flip flops
*undergarments
*sleepwear
*bathing suit and cover up
*cotton blend t-shirts or blouses
*leggings and tunic (optional)
*lightweight, loose-fitting pants
*jeans (if traveling during winter months)
*long shorts (okay for males)
*sweater (optional)

*long, loose skirt for females and nice pants for males if need to dress up during your visit
*sunscreen and hat
*medications
*insect repellent
*raincoat or waterproof jacket/windbreaker
*waterproof bag (to safeguard phone, camera, etc.)
*toiletries and cosmetics
*small packs of tissues (toilet paper is not always in the bathrooms so be sure to carry some tissues with you)
*documents
*cell phone and charger
*camera (optional)
*Kindle or iPad loaded with reading material, travel apps, music, and games (optional)

TERRANCE ZEPKE
Series Reading Order & Guide

Series List

≈

Introduction

Terrance Zepke studied Journalism at the University of Tennessee and later received a Master's degree in Mass Communications from the University of South Carolina. She studied parapsychology at the renowned Rhine Research Center.

Zepke spends much of her time happily traveling around the world but always returns home to the Carolinas where she lives part-time in both states. She has written hundreds of articles and more than fifty books. She is the host of *Terrance Talks Travel: Über Adventures*. Additionally, this award-winning and best-selling author has been featured in many publications and programs, such as NPR, CNN, *The Washington Post,* Associated Press, Travel with Rick Steves, Around the World, *Publishers Weekly,* World Travel & Dining with Pierre Wolfe, *San Francisco Chronicle*, Good Morning Show, *Detroit Free Press*, The Learning Channel, and The Travel Channel.

When she's not investigating haunted places, searching for pirate treasure, or climbing lighthouses, she is most likely packing for her next adventure to some far flung place, such as Reykjavik or Kwazulu Natal. Some of her favorite adventures include piranha fishing on the Amazon, shark cage diving in South Africa, hiking Peru's Inca Trail, camping in the Himalayas, dog-sledding in the Arctic Circle, and a gorilla safari in the Congo.

You can also connect with Terrance on Twitter **@terrancezepke** or on

www.facebook.com/terrancezepke
www.pinterest.com/terrancezepke
www.goodreads.com/terrancezepke

Sign up for weekly email notifications of the ***Terrance Talks Travel*** blog to be the first to learn about new episodes of her travel show, learn cheap travel tips, access dozens of free downloadable TRAVEL REPORTS, and discover her TRIP PICK OF THE WEEK at www.terrancetalkstravel.com or sign up for her ***Mostly Ghostly*** blog and check out her GHOST TOWN at www.terrancezepke.com.

≈

TERRANCE
TALKS
TRAVEL

You can follow her travel show, **TERRANCE TALKS TRAVEL: ÜBER ADVENTURES on www.blogtalkradio.com/terrancetalkstravel** or subscribe to it at **iTunes.**

Warning: Listening to this show could lead to a spectacular South African safari, hot-air ballooning over the Swiss Alps, Disney Adventures, and Tornado Tours!

≈

MOST HAUNTED SERIES

A Ghost Hunter's Guide to the Most Haunted Places in America (2012)
A Ghost Hunter's Guide to the Most Haunted Houses in America (2013)
A Ghost Hunter's Guide to the Most Haunted Hotels & Inns in America (2014)
A Ghost Hunter's Guide to the Most Haunted Historic Sites in America (2016)
The Ghost Hunter's MOST HAUNTED Box Set (3 in 1): Discover America's Most Haunted Destinations (2016)

MOST HAUNTED and SPOOKIEST Sampler Box Set: Featuring *A GHOST HUNTER'S GUIDE TO THE MOST HAUNTED PLACES IN AMERICA* and *SPOOKIEST CEMETERIES* (2017)
A Ghost Hunter's Guide to the Most Haunted Places in the World (2018)

≈

SPOOKIEST SERIES

Spookiest Lighthouses (2013)
Spookiest Battlefields (2015)
Spookiest Cemeteries (2016)
Spookiest Objects (2017) *Spookiest Box Set (3 in 1): Discover America's Most Haunted Destinations* (2016)

≈

TERRANCE TALKS TRAVEL SERIES

Terrance Talks Travel: A Pocket Guide to South Africa (2015)
Terrance Talks Travel: A Pocket Guide to African Safaris (2015)
Terrance Talks Travel: A Pocket Guide to Adventure Travel (2015)
Terrance Talks Travel: A Pocket Guide to Florida Keys (including Key West & The Everglades) (2016)
Terrance Talks Travel: The Quirky Tourist Guide to Key West (2017)
Terrance Talks Travel: The Quirky Tourist Guide to Cape Town (2017)
Terrance Talks Travel: The Quirky Tourist Guide to Reykjavik (2017)
Terrance Talks Travel: The Quirky Tourist Guide to Charleston, South Carolina (2017)
Terrance Talks Travel: The Quirky Tourist Guide to Ushuaia (2017)
Terrance Talks Travel: The Quirky Tourist Guide to Antarctica (2017)
Terrance Talks Travel: The Quirky Tourist Guide to Machu Picchu & Cuzco (Peru) 2017

African Safari Box Set: Featuring TERRANCE TALKS TRAVEL: *A Pocket Guide to South Africa* and *TERRANCE TALKS TRAVEL: A Pocket Guide to African Safaris* (2017)

Terrance Talks Travel: A Pocket Guide to East Africa's Uganda and Rwanda (2018)

Terrance Talks Travel: The Quirky Tourist Guide to Kathmandu (Nepal) & The Himalayas (2018)
Terrance Talks Travel: The Quirky Tourist Guide to Edinburgh (Scotland) (2018)
Terrance Talks Travel: The Quirky Tourist Guide to Marrakesh (Morocco) (2018)

≈

CHEAP TRAVEL SERIES

How to Cruise Cheap! (2017)

How to Fly Cheap! (2017)

How to Travel Cheap! (2017)

How to Travel FREE or Get Paid to Travel! (2017)

CHEAP TRAVEL SERIES (4 IN 1) BOX SET (2017)

≈

STOP TALKING SERIES

Stop Talking & Start Writing Your Book (2015)
Stop Talking & Start Publishing Your Book (2015)
Stop Talking & Start Selling Your Book (2015)
Stop Talking & Start Writing Your Book Series (3 in 1) Box Set (2016)

Message from the Author

The primary purpose of this guide is to introduce you to some titles you may not have known about. Another reason for it is to let you know all the ways you can connect with me. Authors love to hear from readers. We truly appreciate you more than you'll ever know. You're the reason we keep writing! Please feel free to send me a comment or question via the comment form provided on www.terrancezepke.com and www.terrancetalkstravel.com or follow me on your favorite social media. Don't forget that you can also listen to my writing podcast on iTunes, *A Writer's Journey*, or my travel show, **Terrance Talks Travel: Über Adventures** on Blog Talk Radio and iTunes. The best way to make sure you don't miss any episodes of these shows (and find a complete archive of shows), new book releases, giveaways and contests, my TRIP PICK OF THE WEEK, cheap travel tips, and dozens of free downloadable travel reports is to subscribe to ***Terrance Talks Travel*** on www.terrancetalkstravel.com or ***Mostly Ghostly*** on www.terrancezepke.com.

Terrance

P.S. I would like to ask you to take a couple of minutes to share your feedback about any of my books you have read by posting a short review on your favorite bookseller's site so that other readers might discover the title(s) too. This doesn't have to be more than a sentence or two. Authors appreciate readers more than you realize and we dearly love and depend upon your good reviews. Thank you!

INDEX

F

G

H

I

J

K

M

O

P

R

S

T

U

W

Y

Made in the USA
Columbia, SC
31 July 2019